LIVING THE CAMINO BACK HOME

IGNATIAN TIPS FOR KEEPING THE CAMINO SPIRIT ALIVE

Brendan McManus SJ
& Katherine O'Flynn FCJ

Published by Messenger Publications, 2024.

ISBN: 9781788127134
Cover image: Shutterstock.com
Typeset in Adobe Garamond Pro
Design: Brendan McCarthy
Printed b y GPS Colour Graphics

Messenger MJP Publications
www.messenger.ie

Messenger Publications,
37 Leeson Place, Dublin D02 E5V0
www.messenger.ie

The following reflections are based on personal experience on the Camino and on what other pilgrims have shared over the years with us in our work as Camino Companions, a ministry for welcoming pilgrims in Santiago.[1] We noticed that as well as having a space in which to tell their unique Camino stories while in Santiago, pilgrims wanted help to reflect on the importance and relevance for their lives back home (the real Camino!). This book is a suggestion as to what they might do on returning home in terms of keeping that Camino spirit alive. Inevitably it is written from the Christian perspective of its authors, but it can be used by pilgrims of all faiths and none.

1 The Camino Companions initiative is run by the FCJ Sisters and is located on the first floor of the main pilgrim office in Santiago, www.facebook.com/CaminoCompanions.

Introduction

We are all pilgrims in the world and our challenge is to live life as a journey, not buying into the consumer mentality but keeping our hearts open. Back at home we easily forget this and can drift along on autopilot. But we *have a choice* about how we live and love. God (or Mystery, or Spirit) is always with us, and can be seen especially when looking back on our experience. Hence the importance of reflection and taking time out to get perspective. The Camino 'feeling', or the spiritual dimension, is always there, but we have to walk our road of trust as best we can wherever we find ourselves. The 'Camino will provide', even back home, though it is more challenging and needs some supports (see Appendix 1 and 2).

Part of a centuries-old tradition: The Pilgrimage to Santiago de Compostela[2]

The cathedral in Santiago de Compostela is the reputed burial place of St James the Great, one of Jesus' apostles. The Camino, or 'Way of St James', became a major pilgrimage route in medieval times from the tenth century onwards, as an alternative to Rome and Jerusalem. James was one of the Apostles, the brother of John the Evangelist. It is believed that after the Resurrection, the Apostles began to spread the story of Christ, firstly in Jerusalem and then throughout other parts of Palestine and the rest of the then known world, but mainly throughout the region of the Mediterranean Basin. Oral tradition claims that James went to preach in the Iberian Peninsula, and we know that Christianity grew here at a faster rate than elsewhere in western Europe.

There exist various accounts of the transfer of the body of James to Galicia. The most widely held

2 Adapted with permission from 'Spiritual Tour of Part of the Exterior of the Cathedral', January 2024, by Nóirín Uí Mhaolaoí, volunteer with Camino Companions.

version relates how the disciples of James brought his body to the Galician coast, where they disembarked at what is today the village of Padrón. We are told that the disciples moved inland and laid the body to rest in its sepulchre '*sub arcis marmoricis*', believed to refer to the marble arches in a Roman cemetery, where, in the ninth century, the remains of James and his two disciples, Atanasio and Theodoro, were discovered.[3] A monk named Pelagius saw lights appearing in the sky over the area then known as Libredón, where the cemetery was situated. Excavations were carried out and the sepulchres believed to contain the bodies of James and his two disciples were found, in what is known today as Santiago de Compostela.

It was to this site, in the year 834, that King Alfonso II of Asturias travelled from his court in Oviedo. He ordered that a church be built over the shrine containing the remains. Very quickly the numbers of people coming to venerate the tomb became so great that Alfonso III of Asturias ordered a bigger church to be built, but soon that church too became too small. In 1075 building began on the edifice we see in Santiago today. It was completed in 1211.

News of the discovery of the remains of St James in Santiago de Compostela led to huge numbers of pilgrims from all over Europe making the journey

3 This is the account that was widely held in medieval times and was reiterated by Pope Leo XIII in his 1884 Epistle *Deus Omnipotens* concerning 'The Transfer of the Remains of James to Galicia'.

to Santiago. The rapid construction of bridges, pilgrim hospitals and defences along the pilgrim routes across Spain was instrumental in the numbers of pilgrims travelling.

Some pilgrims travelled overland and others, especially those from Ireland, Wales, Scotland, England and the Scandinavian countries travelled by sea. People went on pilgrimage for reasons of devotion; as an act of penance; to implore help in cases of suffering, hardship or ill health etc. Sometimes, people who had committed offences or crimes were ordered, as a form of punishment, to walk the Camino.

In medieval times people went on pilgrimage to gain indulgence, especially plenary indulgence. Indulgences could be gained by almsgiving, by prayer, or by going on pilgrimage to a holy site, such as Santiago de Compostela, which housed the relic of a saint.

Pilgrims from northern European countries, from Ireland, Wales, Scotland, and England made their way to the ports of their own country and then travelled by boat to A Coruña, which is 75 Kilometres directly north of Santiago. Until recent times pilgrims had to make the long and often hazardous return journey back to their own countries, something which we, as modern pilgrims, forget.

The great surge that we see today began after the two world wars, and in the 1950s when French people, especially, began walking. Francisco Franco, during his dictatorship (1939–75), was instrumental in promoting the Camino, especially in the towns and cities along the Camino Francés. The Jubilee Year of 1993 saw great numbers travelling to Santiago de Compostela. This was the beginning of the phenomenon we see today. Access to social media, better health conditions, more free time, ease of travel, emphasis on spirituality and the enjoyment of nature, are, no doubt, factors that contribute to our continued desire to walk this ancient and sacred path. The attraction does not seem to have abated and annual numbers have surpassed pre-pandemic levels, setting new records.[4] The Camino offers something unique as an antidote to our modern technological, consumerist and individualistic society.

A transformative experience

The Camino is a taste of the divine that sets hearts on fire and transforms us, often bringing us 'back to life' after challenging losses or periods of emptiness. When we find ourselves at a crossroads, our experience on the Camino can help us to discern, to find where our hearts are being drawn. The Camino's transformation process is not without its pain. It is

4 Santiago de Compostela's Cathedral Office announced that it recorded 446,035 pilgrims in 2023, underlining the pilgrimage destination's increasing popularity, www.pillarcatholic.com/p/camino-sets-new-record-as-pilgrimages.

often a challenging journey where we meet ourselves on the road, warts and all, and, paradoxically, where we meet God or the divine. It is hard-won, 'costly grace'. As the Santiago saying goes, 'no pain, no glory'. It is precisely through this heroic struggle with limits, sometimes injury and dependence on others that we 'walk through fire' (Isaiah 43:2) to a place of peace and acceptance that money cannot buy. The thing is, once we have tasted it and touched it, we 'burn for its peace' (St Augustine) and want more of this transformative experience. Inevitably, it is the essence of the spiritual life: radical simplicity, solidarity and deep humanity, which results in joy and a great sense of connection. This life is always available to us, not just in Spain, though it is more difficult in a secular, materialistic cultural context.

A vision of how the world could be

The Camino is undoubtedly a special place where magic happens, and miracles take place on a daily basis. It is like an experience of the 'Reign of God', God's dream for the world. This is an alternative vision of how the world could be if people lived the Camino daily, looked out for each other and realised we're all on the same journey. The Camino is a fantastic melting pot of people of every nationality and creed, and miraculously they all get on, finding a way of communicating despite language barriers. On the trail there is no need for pretence or

hierarchy, all are equal. Dressed in common pilgrim clothes, people's humanity and vulnerability is on full display. The experience of staying overnight in an albergue, sleeping in large dormitories without much comfort and sharing meals in common seems to facilitate the process of drawing close to others who are on the same path. Everyone struggles up steep hills, everyone gets tired and dehydrated, everyone has limits. What is extraordinary, however, is the natural way that people create community and help each other.

Camino walkers or pilgrims go out of their way to help anyone injured or in trouble. They share what water or food they have left, give directions and go to great lengths to put someone back on the path, putting others' needs before their own. It is a beautiful thing to see. Nowhere is this better captured than in *I'll Push You*,[5] a heart-wrenching film about two lifelong friends, Justin and Patrick, who did the entire Camino with Patrick (and many others) pushing Justin in a specialised wheelchair. On the Camino there is little 'trivial conversation' or point scoring; people tend to dive straight into the core issues of who people are (not what they have or do) and why they are walking. Often within minutes people are telling complete strangers their deepest secrets and desires. It is truly humbling and inspiring. People respond in the same way, with

5 www.illpushyou.com.

openness and transparency, everybody listening and trying to understand. Compassion and solidarity abound on the Camino.

When the Camino ends in Santiago

It is a special but vulnerable moment when the pilgrims arrive in Santiago, often after a long and challenging walk. Walking into the cathedral square can be very emotional, and pilgrims may feel a mixture of relief, sadness, elation, sorrow, anticlimax, loss and bitter-sweet ambivalence about finishing a special journey and heading back into their daily lives. A dramatic 'de-acceleration' process is experienced at that moment, from the 'high-octane' Camino adrenaline, to the sudden stop and loss of direction as Camino friends go home or disappear into the throngs of people in the city.

Some pilgrims can be disappointed by their experience. Maybe they started the Camino with high expectations of themselves and of others, having heard about others' amazing stories of transformation. Their own stories can be very different, maybe tough and pain filled, and they may wonder why on earth they ever decided to walk. Only gradually will they realise that the Camino did provide something important for them but, crucially, perhaps not what they expected. The Camino teaches some tough insights but support is needed.

As in life, the challenge is to find meaning in the experience, whether it fits with expectations or, as sometimes happens, is a very different reality from what had been imagined. Coming to find meaning in the unexpected can be one of the great gifts of the Camino. Another expectation, especially at the end of the Camino, is of seeing the *botafumeiro*, the great incense thurible swung in the Cathedral at the end of Mass. The *botafumeiro*, with all its mystique and awesomeness, can express the mystery and wonder of the journey. However, one cannot be certain that it will be swung at every Mass and many pilgrims leave disappointed, despite having had a life-changing experience on the Camino. The invitation here is surely to concentrate on the deeper experience and trust that there are other ways of honouring one's life-changing experience.

Those of us who have worked in the Camino Companions office have been privileged to witness and support people at this pivotal moment of arriving in Santiago; there are a lot of tears and strong emotions, and there is a certain vulnerability. People seem to have a great need to share their stories and emotions at this critical stage, though this is only the beginning of the process of going home (this process of understanding what has happened can take months and even years). Many do not avail of this opportunity for one reason or other but still

have a huge need to speak about their experience. Sometimes, pilgrims on their return find themselves very disappointed when their family and friends fail to take their experience seriously. Returning to a difficult life or a life that involves great change is very challenging and pilgrims need some support. Taking time to prepare for this and seeing how the strength gained on the Camino will be there at home can be very important. For some pilgrims, the fact that they actually made it to Santiago despite the many physical, emotional and spiritual challenges can be a wonderful source of strength and confidence in themselves. Winding down expectations can be important in life. The Camino can be a great teacher of this grounding perspective.

The reason for walking

Some pilgrims have a fairly clear motive for walking which has informed their whole pilgrimage: a life transition, a major loss, a promise made to another, a search for meaning etc. Looking at one's own motivation before beginning can be helpful as that can guide when the days are hard, and you wonder if you really want to continue.[6] However, many pilgrims discover that a different motivation may reveal itself as they walk. They may find that the

6 For more on this, see Brendan McManus SJ, *Contemplating the Camino: An Ignatian Guide* (Dublin: Messenger Publications, 2019), section 2, p. 15, 'What Do You Really Want? Preparing for the Camino'.

search for God or the divine is more important than they first acknowledged. Those coming from a very hectic life may discover that they are looking for silence and quiet as they walk. Some pilgrims begin by saying they are walking to experience the culture and history of Spain but, as with the layers of an onion, they discover other deeper motives as they journey. Most pilgrims are normally happy to share this information in a safe space. This 'deep desire' or intention is what defines their experience and, depending on how it has gone, is a source of great joy or sadness. A very helpful practice common to many pilgrims is that of writing a personal diary or journal, as this can be a record of one's changing perceptions, insights, moods and experiences and will help that inner journey of self-discovery. It can also be very valuable when pilgrims go home and want to stay in touch with and deepen their experience.

Understanding that finishing the Camino is just the beginning

This sounds odd, but arriving in Santiago is only 'halfway on the journey',[7] and pilgrims need lots of time and support to unpack and reflect on what has often been a very profound experience. To make the most of this transformation, and not leave it in Spain, they have to figure out a way of keeping it

7 Alexander John Shaia, *Returning From Camino* (Santa Fe, NM: Journey of Quadratos, 2nd Edition, 2019).

alive in their hearts, which is not so easy when they are back in the reality and pressures of their lives. Having had these significant experiences, they need to express them, put them into words and be heard. Even among their fellow pilgrims they may not have had a chance to say what is really going on for them, and they are often ready and open for some reflection. The other side of it is that back at home, friends or family who have not had the experience tire of hearing these 'incredible' Camino stories. Alexander John Shaia recommends getting a spiritual director or guide who will listen to and help them with this reflection process and how to integrate this into their lives at home. Ironically, this process can often take months and even years, as pilgrims unpack and understand the depth of spiritual experience and what it means for their lives.

The process of unpacking the Camino takes a lot longer than unpacking a backpack. There can be a certain inverse investment of time at the beginning and at end of the Camino. Many pilgrims take great care and time in physical preparation and choosing what to put in their backpacks before they begin, but at the end, what is left in the backpack is quickly disposed of. The temptation is to rush into the next experience, while 'unpacking' requires a process of time and reflection. At the same time, there can be much less preparation for the inner journey at the beginning, but hopefully the experience can be unpacked reverently and gradually at the end and when pilgrims return home. The key thing, however, is that *pilgrims must never doubt the importance of what has happened on the Camino* and should trust their pilgrim experience, even in the face of apparent apathy, cynicism and begrudging secularism.

The need to be listened to

The most important thing you need is attentive, intentional listening and a safe space where you can tell your story, in your own way, without being interrupted. This is a 'sacred space',where you can reveal personal thoughts and feelings in confidence. A further step is trying to help you to process the multi-layered Camino experience, which takes time and trust. You need someone without an agenda asking *open* questions that help to go a bit deeper, for example: What does this experience mean for your life? What experience stays with you, what did you take home with you? What will you do differently now that you are back home? What is God or the Spirit saying to you through this? Unfortunately, many of the people in our lives are not trained in this and are often not great listeners, hence, the need to seek out a person or a group that can provide this space (see ideas at the end). People who have not had the Camino experience often don't really understand what it means, and you can expect eyes glazing over and a loss of interest. It can be helpful to be very intentional about seeking the right place: for example, have a 'soul friend' (*anam cara* in Gaelic), a spiritual director, a faith-sharing group or a Camino group so that you can talk about what has happened and reverence the experience.

Understanding what has happened on the Camino as spiritual

People often need help understanding their Camino experience in terms of a 'spirituality of everyday life'. Many pilgrims will tell you very quickly that they are spiritual, not religious. They have often had negative experiences of religion or unhelpful images of God or external 'magical' spirituality, with excessive focus on miracles and external events. As a result, they are slow to recognise that what is happening *inside* them, in their experience, is of God/mystery/spirit. It can often be a great liberation and relief to realise that their Camino experience, a profound encounter with the deepest parts of themselves, is the work of God who is active there. What often features in their stories are really challenging moments and reaching limits (of energy, patience, courage), and managing to walk though these moments and into some deeper place where peace and healing exists. They just need to know they don't have to be perfect or 'holy'. Rather, amazingly, God is in the 'mess' with them.[8]

Pilgrims will often talk of the spirituality found in nature, whether gazing quietly at the beauty all around them or finding themselves touched by the simplicity of tiny flowers and even ants. Stopping for a brief moment of quiet in a wayside chapel is important for many pilgrims, whether they have faith or not. Somehow these holy places touch a deep place. Pilgrims also frequently discover their amazing capacity for perseverance in dealing with injuries and physical pain on the Camino. These can sometimes be considered as merely physical and as having nothing to do with God or the spiritual. One of gifts of the Camino is the capacity to see ourselves in a holistic way and realise that our physical injuries and pain are not separate from our spiritual selves. The spiritual life is not confined to religious rituals.

Something significant always happens on the Camino – from tourist to pilgrim

The Camino always touches people at some level, regardless of their belief or lack of it. Many pilgrim stories feature the paradox that while the initial purpose might have been a good walk, time with friends, a cheap holiday, they are in some way changed by the experience. Some say that inside

8 Jim Deeds & Brendan McManus SJ, *Finding God in the Mess* (Dublin: Messenger Publications, 2023).

every so-called 'Camino tourist', a fledgling pilgrim lies hidden. The walking for long hours, being out in nature, the natural contemplation that occurs, the images, memories and emotions of life coming to the surface, enable this movement from tourist to pilgrim. People tend to live this introspection intensely, even though it doesn't feel like effort on the trail. The absence of distractions, the simplicity of having all you need on your back, lack of exposure to technology, meeting people who are ready to engage in a deeper way and long periods of time alone brings people into contact with themselves. Thus, the rewards are great, as they literally walk out and work out problems that their bodies know the answer to (and their heads don't). It is integrated head and heart living (an 'incarnated spirituality'[9]), dealing with the important and often messy issues of life, which is the real stuff. When they can manage this pilgrims often talk about great feelings of peace, tranquillity and joy. It is indeed a great loss if this experience is not integrated into post-Camino life. The great guidebook writer, John Brierley, who died recently, was very aware of this and often spoke of the importance of taking the Camino back into life.[10] Again, people need a framework or spirituality for understanding their Camino experience that will

9 Andy Otto, 'The Incarnation is at Hand', *God in All Things* (website), https://godinallthings.com/2017/12/22/the-incarnation-is-at-hand/.

10 Greg Daly, 'Bringing the Camino Home', *The Irish Catholic*, 4 April 2019, www.irishcatholic.com/bringing-the-camino-home/.

help them live it out daily.

The humanising effect of the Camino

The Camino brings people in touch with their basic humanity and connection to others. It is the great equaliser or leveller, as everyone is equal on the road and it doesn't matter who you are or what your background is. Few pilgrims on the trail ask others about their careers or 'status' back home, while one of the most frequent questions is 'How are your feet?' This is what matters on the Camino, and pilgrims quickly come to appreciate the common humanity shared by all, regardless of language, creed, financial status and culture. Pilgrims learn the importance of tolerating difference, relating well to others, having compassion and not judging. A lot of Camino stories revolve around the importance of hospitality and welcome; as pilgrims arriving in a new place, they are often tired, hungry and worn out, so how people treat them matters a great deal. The generosity of local people who reach out day after day to pilgrims, the kindness of *hospitalarias/os* and the solidarity of other pilgrims renews belief in the goodness of humanity. 'Com-passion' is literally feeling for the suffering of another in our shared humanity. This is often difficult but not impossible to recreate in modern society. Returning from the Camino, we are invited to bring that compassion and solidarity with humanity into our families, our places of work and life in general.

Learning how to be really free

Pilgrims often report that mistakes, injuries or wrong turns have been the greatest learning points. This points to the value of the unexpected, the providential and the 'uncontrollable'. In fact, letting go of control (called spiritual freedom[11]) is one of the most challenging and, ironically, one of the most rewarding aspects. Experience is hard earned on the Camino and unfortunately there are no shortcuts. The Camino has to be fully lived and experienced, both in its ups and in its downs. Injuries and pain can teach us to slow down, to let go of control and to let God and others help us. God is no longer perceived as a strict and distant disciplinarian. The God of compassion is discovered through one's own vulnerability. Some pilgrims take days off, albeit at times reluctantly, to deal with injuries and pain, and in doing so, they learn to become more reflective and more accepting of their vulnerability and, consequently, the vulnerability of others. These days off can be just as important as the long days of walking. People need help to see the value of these seemingly negative or 'disastrous' experiences (God in all things) as learning or growth experiences.

11 James Hanvey SJ, 'Finding freedom with Ignatius', *Thinking Freedom* (website), www.thinkingfaith.org/articles/finding-freedom-st-ignatius.

Similarly, this letting go of control and being open to learning as a pilgrim in life, is an important attitude to maintain.

The need to keep your pilgrim heart alive

Going back home can sometimes be a step back into comfort, routine, apathy and lethargy. We have to keep our pilgrim hearts open by not getting caught up in the 'small stuff', such as boredom, distraction and fatigue, and keeping on the move: muscles are sore for a day, but beauty lasts for ever. Seeing the early morning sunrise (always available to us), dappled sunlight in a brook, a riot of wild flowers, all make a lasting impression that speaks to our hearts. Having a heart that is full and sings, vastly outweighs any minor irritations and strains that modern life brings. Unfortunately, people can sometimes prioritise the second over the first; in order not to push ourselves or feel any pain we no longer receive any joy and fail to appreciate the wonder and awe of being alive. The simplicity of the Camino, having what we need on our backs, sharing what we have with others, teaches us that possessions will not bring happiness. Many pilgrims decide to declutter when they return home as a means of keeping that simplicity alive in their hearts.

We need a space to keep Camino memories alive and that often means returning to what was

nourishing and life-giving for us. This is another reason why photos and mementos are important; keeping a Camino journal can be a great help afterwards. Returning to those precious insights and experiences can be a way of savouring what gives us life. Remembering and relishing what has been good and positive is another Ignatian practice that we can build in to life. The Assyrian proverb 'tell me who your friends are and I'll tell you who you are' reminds us that we become like those around us. If we are to keep our hearts full and open to life, we need to be around people who will also live every day as pilgrims, people who see beyond the material and often cynical world, people who will help us get beyond the 'small stuff' and so live full lives.

Keep your eyes in the path ahead

One thing that has helped Camino pilgrims back home to not be overwhelmed is to focus on the 'path' ahead, the realisation that we can live only one day at a time. The Camino teaches people this, to live in the moment and not to plan too far ahead. We need only one plan for the day, one set of clothes, one meal at a time, one foot in front of the other. It is a radical simplicity. Modern life frustrates and complicates; it is inherently focused on the future and is anxiety inducing. It has us face multiple options, as if we could cram fifty options into a day, and we end up doing justice to none of them; a dull frustration ensues. We need to work hard to remember this

simple insight; just work out what step we need to take next without over-thinking things. Learning to trust and leaving the future in God's hands is a lifelong lesson. As on the Camino, we don't know if we will have the courage to keep going when the road is hard, how our bodies will cope with the ups and downs, the heat and the rain, the uncertainty and risk. The poet Jan Richardson puts it like this:

If we could see the journey whole, we might never undertake it …

Call it one of the mercies of the road,

that we only see it by stages as it opens up before us.[12]

12 Jan Richardson, 'For Those Who Have Far To Travel, An Epiphany Blessing', in *Circle of Grace: A Book of Blessings for the Seasons* (Orlando, FL: Wanton Gospeller Press, 2015).

Trust the yellow arrows – discern your choices

The yellow arrows are a wonderful support on the Camino. They guide us across mountains and through bustling cities and sprawling villages. It is not so easy in life to find yellow arrows at every crossroads. We have to discern our choices in prayer and reflection and see where God is drawing us. This takes time and trust, but we know that, just as surely as the arrow will appear on the Camino, God will let us know what path to take.

We are always faced with choices and we need consistently to 'choose life'. A key spiritual insight is that there are two 'voices' speaking to us at any moment: one is from God and leads to life, while the other is called the 'enemy of human nature' and leads to 'death'. While this is primarily a spiritual insight, it obviously has huge implications for mental health and psychological well-being. Ultimately, it boils down to consistently making life-enhancing decisions (i.e. following the yellow arrows), tackling the seductive demons and unmasking them. In the Ignatian tradition, there is a whole system for differentiating the voices, known as discernment of spirits,[13] to help people be wise to the deceptions and attempts at sabotage.

Remember – you are not just an individual but part of a long tradition of pilgrimage

Some pilgrims take great delight in knowing that they are part of a huge throng of people who have walked to Santiago for over a thousand years. Being conscious of this is quite counter-intuitive in our individualistic culture and it helps to put our sometimes arrogant twenty-first-century view of ourselves in perspective. This can also help when we return home as we see ourselves as belonging to something greater than our family, our town or city or our country. While we may walk alone on the Camino, we are never alone. There are always others somewhere on the journey and there are

13 Joseph A. Tetlow SJ, 'Discernment in a Nutshell', *Ignatian Spirituality* (website of Loyola Press), www.ignatianspirituality.com/making-good-decisions/discernment-of-spirits/discernment-in-a-nutshell/.

those multitudes who have walked in the past. The Camino family is constantly growing.

The Camino Companions

The FCJ Sisters (Faithful Companions of Jesus) recognised the need to provide a welcome space for pilgrims in Santiago in 2015. The Association of Dutch Pilgrims and the German bishops had already established places of welcome for pilgrims coming from the Netherlands and Germany. Mass in English was available for English-speaking pilgrims, but there was no 'space' where pilgrims could gather throughout the day to talk about what had happened, share their experiences and reflect on their Camino. The dean of the cathedral encouraged the FCJ sisters to provide this opportunity for English-speaking pilgrims and offered a corridor room adjacent to the office where pilgrims received their 'Compostela', the certificate awarded to those who walk at least 100 km on one of the Camino routes. The sisters quickly recognised that this physical meeting place had also a much more important psychological and spiritual implication, as pilgrims were given 'space' to reflect, share and be listened to at the end of their Camino. In 2017 a new International Pilgrim Centre was opened in Santiago. This enabled all the language groups, including the French, to have a more spacious private room where they could

welcome pilgrims. In 2023, a welcome room for Spanish pilgrims was established by the Jesuits.

Throughout the past nine years, except for the Covid-19 years of 2020 and 2021, the FCJ sisters have been present in Santiago from Easter to the end of October. They offer this service with the support and help of generous volunteers, mostly former pilgrims, who desire to give back to the Camino. Several lay women and some men, many religious from other congregations, FCJ lay associates (Companions in Mission), diocesan priests and ordained ministers from various congregations have offered their time and gifts to welcome and to be available to pilgrims. They come from a variety of Christian denominations and many different countries and collaborate with a Filipino priest, a Camino aficionado, Fr Manny Domingo SDB, who celebrates Mass in English each day in the small chapel at the Pilgrims' Office.

Walking the Camino for a week, a month or several months, having no agenda other than to walk to the next overnight stop, empties the mind of clutter and opens the pilgrim up to new dimensions, including the spiritual. The support of other pilgrims often provides a kind of family atmosphere and strong bonds develop. Consequently, ending this experience on arrival in Santiago, can be disconcerting and confusing for some pilgrims as they say goodbye to their new-found friends and the freedom of the road. They are grateful for a place to pause, reflect and make the transition back to their families, work etc. Camino Companions provides a liminal space where pilgrims can make the transition from the experience of Camino to the next phase of their lives. Pilgrims who return to challenging situations appreciate the opportunity to name what lies ahead and draw on the insights of the Camino and what it has taught them.

To facilitate this process, the Camino Companions offer a safe and welcoming space for the sharing of stories, quiet reflection and encountering fellow pilgrims in Santiago de Compostela. This is responding to a need for pilgrims to share their experiences, debrief a little and prepare for the return to post-Camino life. People can be in very different places on finishing the Camino. Some find arriving in Santiago an anticlimax and need space to come to terms with what their Camino has meant for them. Sometimes, pilgrims just want to laugh, share and enjoy the great memories together at the end of the Camino. Either way, people need help to validate and integrate their experience, and support for continuing the journey back at home. The Camino Companions, many of whom are spiritual directors or guides, help by lending a listening ear and letting people talk about their unique Camino experience.

46

It is very flexible – people can drop in and have a quick chat or, if they want to deepen the experience, there are more structured Camino reflection sessions for individuals and groups.

A framework for processing pilgrim experience

Walking the path of life, our personal Camino, it can be helpful to take time to look back, reflect and understand our inner experience in terms of finding the way ahead. Some of the insights of Ignatian spirituality have proved helpful here as it focuses on finding God in experience, and offers practical techniques to help pilgrims process or interpret their Camino experience. It comes from the prototypical pilgrim, Ignatius Loyola, who criss-crossed Europe alone and on foot, often limping. He developed his insights about God and the world into a series of 'spiritual exercises' that could be done on the move. Ironically, it was a serious injury that precipitated Ignatius's awareness of his contrasting inner moods, leading to his uncovering God's movements *within* his experience. Ignatius was not an enclosed monk but a 'holy itinerant'; he learned to trust in God's providence and care, even though it meant exposure to the accompanying hardships and tribulations. Ignatius learned the necessity of 'letting go, letting God', trusting that things would work out, and handing over decisions and doubts. His idea was to make pilgrims of us all; people who are at home on the road, and who can find God in the places and people they meet. He wanted us to be reflective, discerning agents of God's will in the world. Engaging with the world and critiquing, we are to imitate Christ in his 'Way' or Camino towards God.

The challenge is to be 'awake' and attentive to the urgings of the Spirit and to follow them. God works in our interior moods and feelings, and we can pick up that same 'Camino feeling' (a full heart) to find where God is leading, though we need inner silence and time to listen to our hearts. Our job is to be 'light' in the world (Camino 'angels'), to help others and to give something back. This can be hard when the prevailing culture is one of individualism, ego and self-focus. However, there are ways to structure our lives to make sure that we have pauses, time out and reflection built in so that we can remain close to God by following certain practices (see Appendix 1 and 2). As on the Camino, there will be moments of darkness or suffering, which are a 'testing in the fire' that allows us to face our demons and humbly find a way forward with God's help (handing over control and trusting). We need to seek humility, especially letting go of the need to control.

Don't leave this awesome experience in Spain

Finally, there is a great temptation to think that these

exceptional experiences only happen on the Camino in Spain and that people can't take them home with them. One solution seems to be to keep coming back and doing the Camino obsessively, but this is to deny the lasting significance of these experiences. Hence the importance of finding ways to bring this experience home and integrating some of this learning into life. This was such a common issue for pilgrims who visited the Camino Companions that we put together a sheet of suggestions as how they might do this (see Appendix 1 and 2).

CA
SAN

Appendix 1: Bringing the Camino Home – Some general 'rules of thumb'

Remember that there is a process of adjustment to be gone through. On returning home you may initially feel like a fish out of water. The surrounding consumerism and capitalism can be painful at first, given that you have had a very different experience of how the world can be. Be gentle with yourself.

- Live simply. Give away everything you don't need, have a great clear-out (remember you are pilgrim).
- People first, things second.
- Limit your exposure to technology, increase your time in nature.
- Be brave; don't give in to fear or 'small thinking' (feel the fear and do it anyway).
- Live in your body, exercise or walk out problems, practise awareness (live in the heart, not the head).
- Resist the temptation to control everything, hand things over to God.
- Live in the uncertainty and emotion of situations; believe that the Camino provides, even at home.
- Resist the temptation to resolve everything with a credit card (live with uncertainty).
- See the best in people and give them the benefit of the doubt.

- Help everyone you can (be a Camino angel even if others are not).
- Don't judge before you know the whole story; most people are doing the best they can within their limits.
- Look out for the 'yellow arrows' or signs that will give you direction.
- See every day as a new journey where you will learn humility and be challenged; keep open to the wisdom that life continually teaches.
- Do your 'inner work', i.e. reflection and self-knowledge, which makes you free from addictions and compulsions.

Senda Santa Teodosia
Santa Teodosia 3,3 km. – 1h 10'
1,2 km. – 18'

Appendix 2: Some Practical Ignatian Suggestions

There is some God-given desire or fire within us that we have experienced on the Camino, which seeks expression in our daily lives and is where our peace lies. Our goal is to become fully alive and human, just like Jesus was, by tuning in to our inner world of feelings and desires. These are the signs, or 'yellow arrows', that help to orient our lives. We are called to live like Christ (the ultimate pilgrim), tuning in to God's desire for us and how we could serve the world as pilgrims.

1. Do a 'Review of the Day' or Ignatian 'Examen'[14] at the end of each day. It takes about fifteen minutes to review the day and see where the 'Camino moments' were or where we missed them. The key insight is that by taking some time to reflect or look back on the complex and often hectic experience of our day, we see things differently, often becoming aware of things we have missed and appreciating the gift that is each day. We begin with trying to find gratitude within us for everything good that has happened; this helps shift often habitual negativity towards a more hopeful way of seeing that is more

14 Brendan McManus SJ, 'Examen: the Paradox of Reflection', *Jesuits in Ireland* (website), https://jesuit.ie/blog/brendan-mcmanus/examen-the-paradox-of-reflection.

divine. The five steps of the method are:
i) **Ask God for light**: Try to see the day through God's eyes, not merely your own. See what stands out.
ii) **Give thanks**: Get in touch with gratitude for the day you have just lived as a gift from God. This can be a struggle, as negativity can dominate, but there is always some light to focus on.
iii) **Review the day chronologically:** Look back on the day just completed, being guided by the Spirit. You can often be surprised about all the things you did and people you met, and you may have forgotten much.
iv) **Face your mistakes or shortcomings:** Face up to what is wrong – accept mistakes; work out what you would do better to improve.
v) **Look foward to the next day**: Ask God for help to live a better day – commit yourself to learn and improve.

2. **First thing in the day meditate or pray for around fifteen minutes.** This transition from sleep to wakefulness is sacred, so protect it. Like a cell phone, we need to be 'plugged in' to the source on a daily basis if we are to be alive and well engaged with life. We need some personal prayer practice to keep us grounded and connected to the source. It also works well to go for a walk first thing ('get out of bed

and put on the boots,' as one pilgrim said) to orient ourselves for the day. Remember that prayer is also listening, so create a space and maybe use nature, poetry or scripture to hear what God is saying to us.

3. **Develop an 'attitude of gratitude'**. Our culture favours ingratitude (Ignatius says this is the greatest distortion); we need to be more attentive to the giftedness of life which reflects our origin (created by God) and the ways that God works in our lives. A key Camino insight is seeing everything as a gift, lowering expectations and looking for the good in everything. This also means not prejudging people but assuming that there is good in everyone.

4. **Take time to discern and work through decisions,[15] especially important ones**. You always have a choice about how you deal with events and how you live your life. The 'yellow arrows' or signs are always there but we have to search for them. It is about identifying what is the unhelpful inner movement (anxiety, shame and paralysis, i.e. desolation) and moving towards a more positive one (connection, reconciliation and positive action, i.e. consolation). God or the divine is normally calling us through our humanity, our deeper feelings, not in

15 'An Ignatian Framework for Making a Decision', *Ignatian Spirituality* (website of Loyola Press), www.ignatianspirituality.com/making-good-decisions/an-approach-to-good-choices/an-ignatian-framework-for-making-a-decision/?amp.

huge 'miracles' or external things. Don't make any quick, rushed decisions.

5. **Try to be your 'best Camino self' every day**, to be the person God wants you to be, treating others well, having good healthy relationships and having a goal/direction in life. What often prevents us from being our best selves is being overly attached to particular outcomes or letting self-centredness or the ego rule. For example, we could have certain unhealthy addictions, could be overly self-centred, or could be trying to bargain with God. Therefore, we need to know what our blocks or attachments are in order to be able to work/pray with them, to be really free to do what situations require of us. Stop trying to control things. Try to help others whenever you can; be a 'Camino angel'.

6. **Think about having a 'soul friend'**, spiritual guide, '*anam cara*' or someone to whom you can talk regularly about things that matter. This process of reflection with another pilgrim or companion enables you to look back with a little bit of objectivity. Having a spiritual director or guide (a trained listener) helps you to put things outside yourself, to get perspective and clarity on your inner life. There is much wisdom in this and it helps people to move forward spiritually and be a pilgrim daily.

7. **Keep a spiritual diary or notebook**[16] to record important events and help you reflect on them. Again, it is about tuning in to those important and sacred 'Camino' moments in our lives. We are trying to put into words those things that moved us or were significant. As on the Camino these are our moments of encounter with God or the divine. Although it is challenging to articulate such sublime experiences, which are always there, this can help us discern how God is meeting us or leading us in our prayer.

8. **Think about doing a spiritual retreat or Camino walk** once a year to keep on track. An Ignatian retreat is just like a Camino experience; we leave behind the noisy world and begin an inner journey in which God takes the lead and will open our eyes so that we can see our deepest truth. This type of journey, which has its challenges, allows you to discover the treasure that you are. Finding inner peace and stillness is the goal: 'Be still and know that I am God' (Psalm 46:10). Some retreat centres use walking and bodywork to help you find God and experience that 'Camino feeling'. Find a local prayer group, parish, Camino group or spiritual/retreat centre that can help you.

16 Kevin O'Brien SJ, 'Review Prayer by Keeping a Journal', *Ignatian Spirituality* (website of Loyola Press), www.ignatianspirituality.com/ignatian-prayer/the-what-how-why-of-prayer /review-prayer-by-keeping-a-journal/?amp.

9. **Keep up some sort of spiritual reading and watch some Camino films** or read some pilgrim books to keep your pilgrim soul alive:

Camino films

Martin Sheen's *The Way* (2010)
Walking the Camino: Six Ways to Santiago (2013)
Footprints: The Path of Your Life (2016)
Road to Santiago (*El final del Camino*) (2009)
Camino Skies (2019)
Looking For Infinity: El Camino (2017)
O Apostolo (*The Apostle*) (2012)
I'll Push You (2016)
Phil's Camino (2016)
Camino, The Journey to Santiago (2012)

Camino books

Kevin Codd, *Field of Stars*
Guy Thatcher, *A Journey of Days*
Cees Nooteboom, *Roads to Santiago*
Brendan McManus SJ, *Redemption Road*
Robert C. Sibley, *The Way of the Stars*
Mary O´Hara Wyman, *Grandma's on the Camino*
Jean-Christie Ashmore, *Camino de Santiago: To Walk Far, Carry Less*
Joyce Rupp, *Walk in a Relaxed Manner: Life Lessons from the Camino*
Brendan McManus SJ, *The Road to Manresa*
Brendan McManus SJ, *Brothers in Arms*

10: Live life as a pilgrimage. We are all pilgrims in

the world and only passing through, but it is easy to get attached to things and believe the illusion of the material world. It goes without saying that you have to let go of a lot to be a pilgrim, and walking the Camino is the modern equivalent. As on the Camino so in life; we have to travel light and adapt to whatever comes our way, whether it is the weather, health issues, unexpected obstacles or inner wounds or blocks. Many of these things are beyond our control; leaving control aside and trusting in providence is the only way to live. Therefore, focus on your own path, keep your eyes on the road, don't think too far ahead, and trust that good things will happen. Especially don't let fear rule, it is not a good guide.

To journey without being changed is to be a nomad. To change without journeying is to be a chameleon. To journey and be transformed by the journey is to be a pilgrim.[17]

17 Mark Nepo, *The Book of Awakening: Having the Life You Want by Being Present to the Life You Have* (Newburyport, MA: Red Wheel/Weiser, 2000).